Frog Art Coloring Book

Volume One

Artwork by
Children Around the World

For

FROGS are GREEN

Written by Susan E. Newman
Edited by Mark Lerer

MY FAT FOX LTD
MMXVI

My Fat Fox
86 Gladys Dimson House
London E7 9DF
United Kingdom

www.myfatfox.co.uk

Cover design ©2016 Susan E. Newman

Frog Art Coloring Book Volume One ©2016 Frogs Are Green

ISBN   978-1-905747-49-8

This book is dedicated to frog-lovers of all ages. May you be inspired both environmentally and creatively to do your part in helping to save frogs and amphibians.

Susan E. Newman,
Founder,
Frogs Are Green Inc.

Children's art from around the world

Every Fall, Frogs Are Green invites children to create frog art through drawing, painting, sculpture, collage and photography. Now we've asked them to help us create our first series of coloring books and they've answered! This is the first volume of a series of coloring books we have created from the pictures they sent us.

Thanks to you all for your artwork!

Some images have been edited slightly to make them more suitable for coloring.

List of artists

Frogs have been on the Earth for over 200 million years,
at least as long as the dinosaurs.

Zion Alburo

9 years old
Haledon, New Jersey USA

'Amazon Horned Frog'

Zion Alburo

Toads are frogs, but not all frogs are toads. Both frogs and toads live near ponds, swamps and marshes. Frogs can live on the ground or in trees but toads live only on the ground.

Aiden

6 years old
'Frogs and Flies'

Aiden

Frogs usually have webbed hind feet and some have webbed front feet. Some frogs, such as tree frogs, have pads on their toes that help them climb trees or even to stick to a glass window.

Irtaza Azhar

12 years old
PS 23, Jersey City, NJ USA

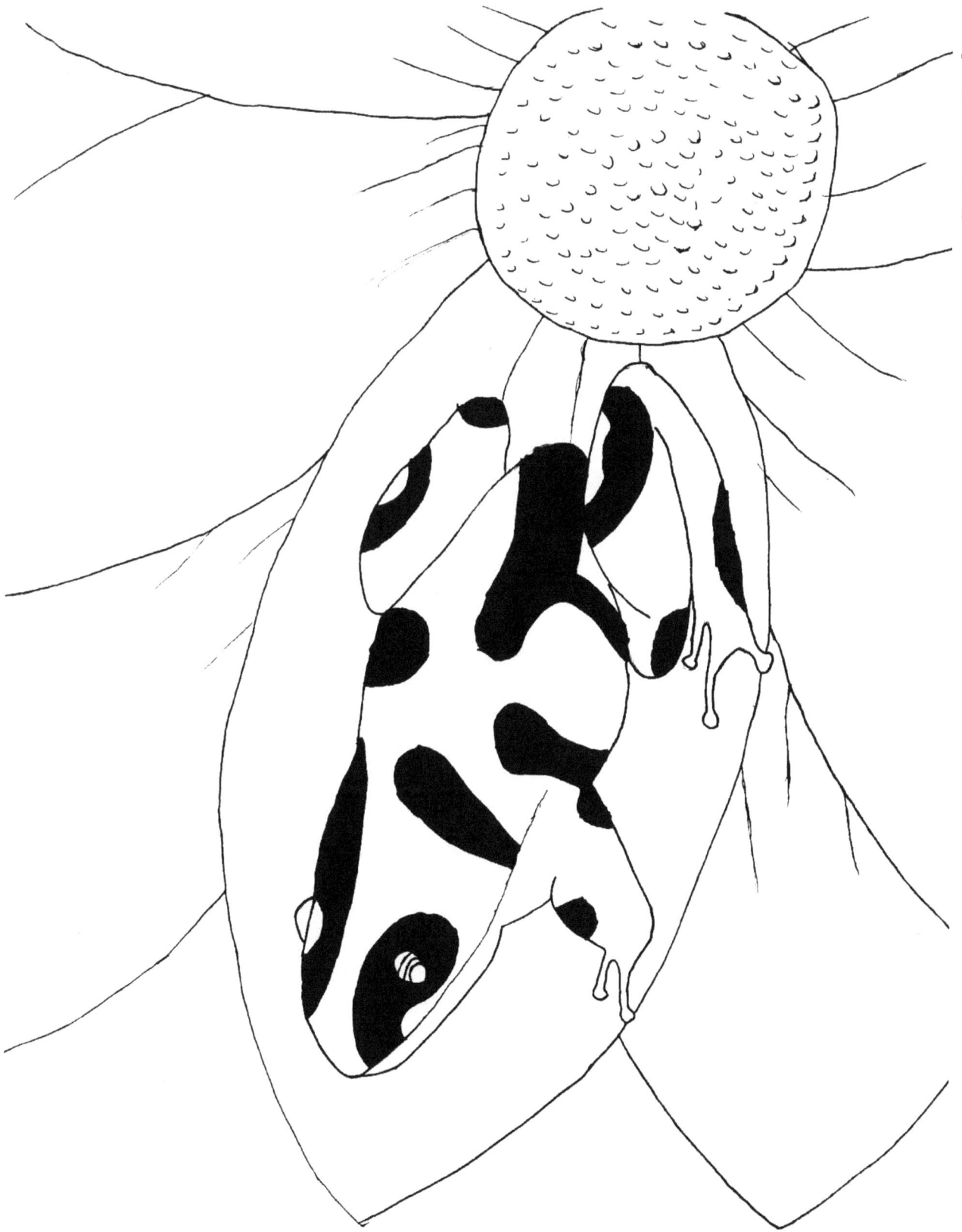

Irtaza Azhar

The largest frog is the African Goliath Frog. One of the smallest frogs, *Paedophryne amanuensis,* which was recently discovered in Papua New Guinea, is smaller than a dime.

AS

Soaring Heights Charter School
New Jersey USA

There are over 6,000 species of frogs worldwide. They exist on all continents except Antarctica.

Xin Yee Lee

12 years old
SJKC Sin Min A.
Kedah
Malaysia

Xin Yee Lee

Some frogs, such as the Dart Frog, secrete poisons through their skin; a single drop could kill a human. Poisonous frogs have bright colors.

Vrishas Bolukonda

5 years old
India

STOP POLLUTION
SAVE GREEN...

Vrishas 15.2.16

Vrishas Bolukonda

Frogs have big, bulging eyes and excellent night vision. Even though they cannot turn their heads, they can see almost 360 degrees around. They also use their eyes to help them swallow food by pushing their eyes down.

Zaniab Ali

12 years old
MS 4
Jersey City
New Jersey USA

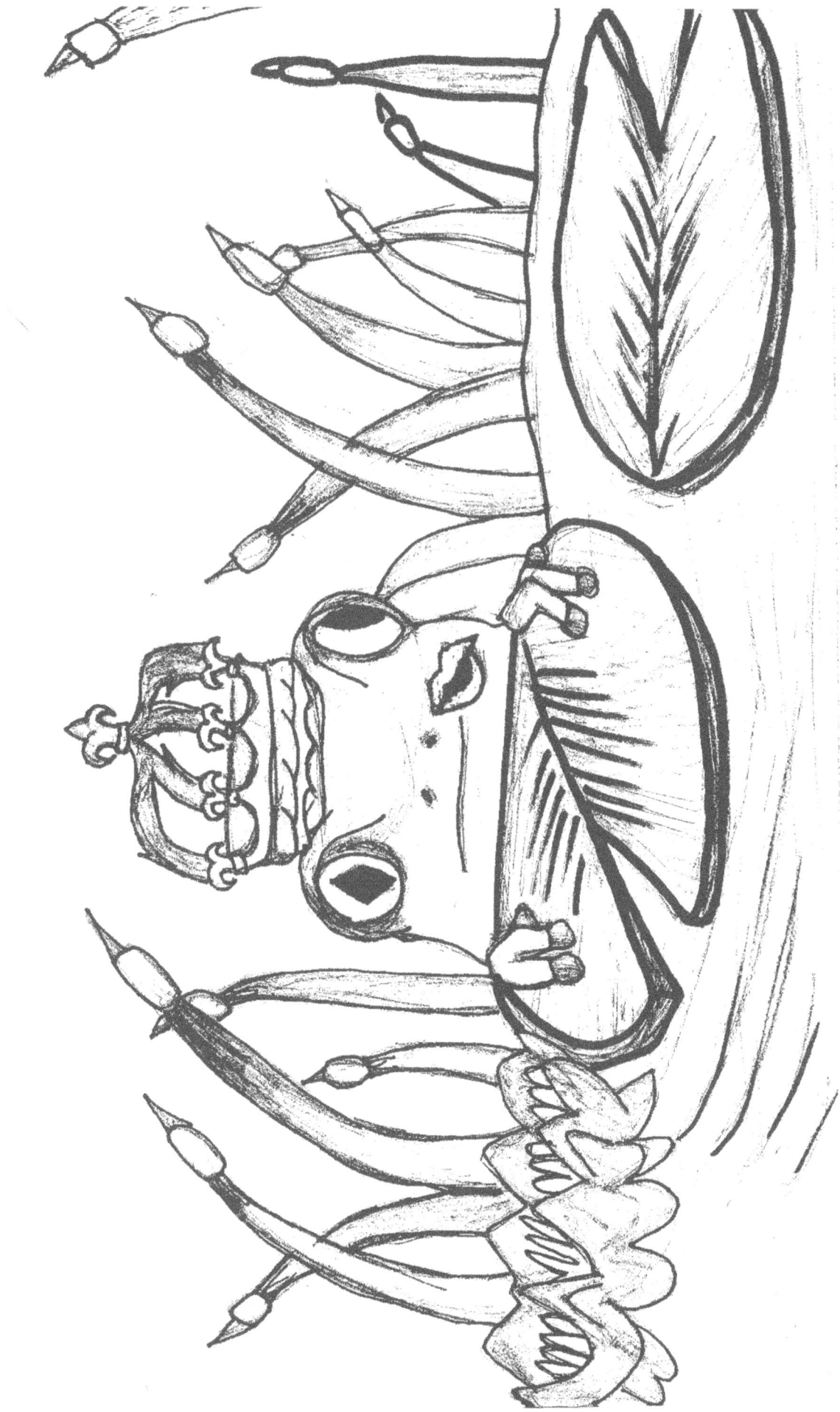

Zaniab Ali

Frogs are cold-blooded. This means their body temperature changes with the temperature of their surroundings. When it gets cold, some frogs dig burrows underground or in the mud at the bottom of ponds and hibernate until spring.

A.B.

SHCS in USA
'Greener Frogs'

A.B.

Many frogs have incredible camouflage. Some have muddy brown, spotty, bumpy skin to help them hide in moss and leaves – and to even hide on trees.

Angel Barachiel S. Muňoz

11 years old
Zamboanga City
Philippines

'Conserve Frogs, Water and the Earth'

Angel Barachiel S. Muñoz

Male frogs call to attract the females. They have vocal sacs - pouches of skin that fill with air like balloons. The balloons act as amplifiers and some frog sounds can be heard a mile away.

Atile Ileviciute

11 years old
Kaunas Art Gymnasium
Lithuania

During mating season, the male frogs in a group will croak quite loudly to attract females. When a female hears a croak she likes, the male will grab her and she will release eggs for him to fertilize.

Xin Yee Lee

12 years old
SJKC Sin Min A.
Kedah
Malaysia

Xin Yee Lee

A frog will eat any living thing that will fit in its mouth. This includes bugs, spiders, worms, slugs, larvae and even small fish.

Kira Alburo

6 years old
New Jersey USA

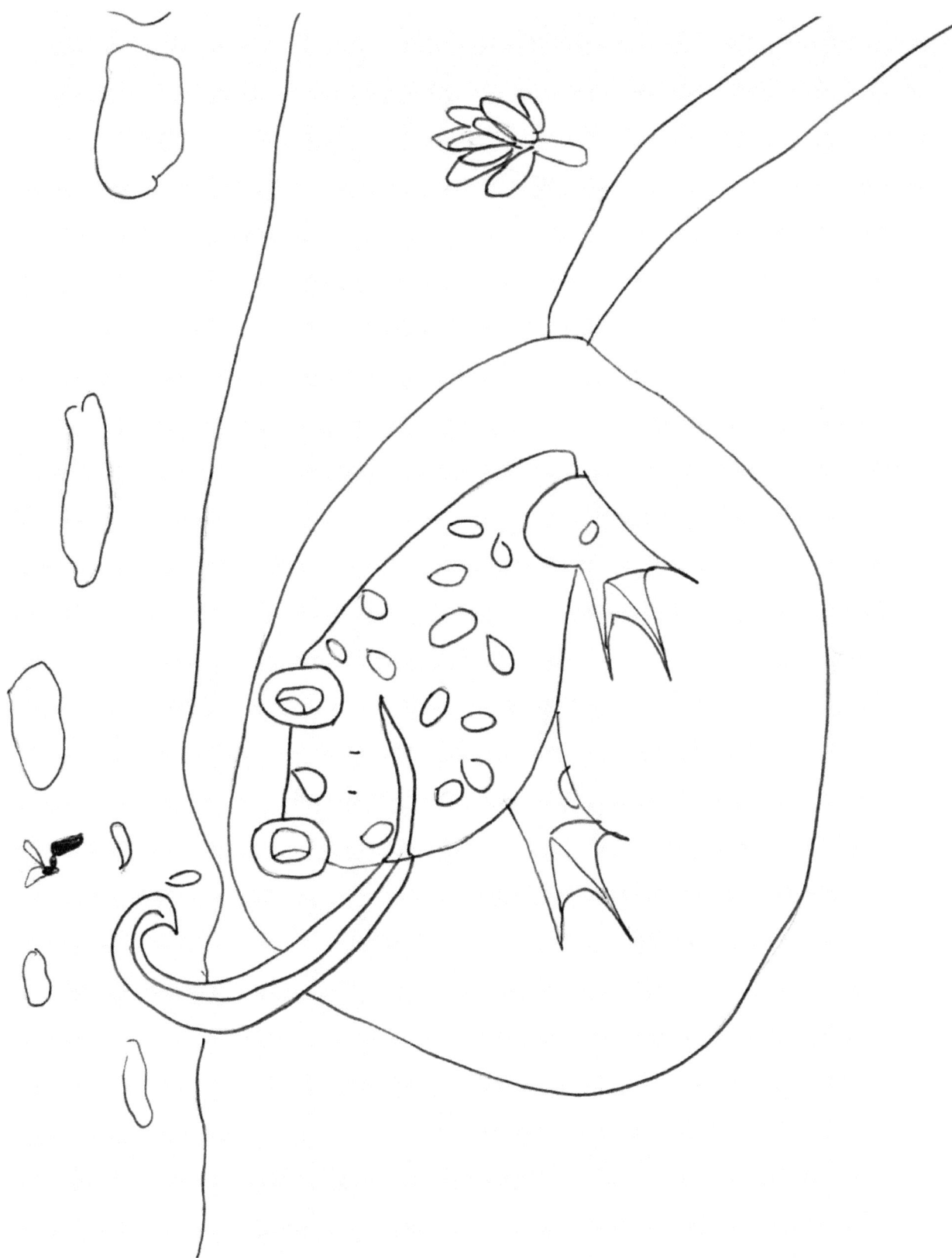

Kira Alburo

To catch prey, the frog's sticky tongue darts out and pulls the prey into its mouth. A frog's tongue can snap back into its mouth within 15/100ths of a second.

Leo Haro

Age unknown
PS23
Jersey City
New Jersey USA

Leo Haro

Frogs are social creatures that live in groups. A group of frogs is called an army, colony or knot. Groups of frogs will even swim together in schools like fish.

Esmerelda Garcia

14 years old
PS23
Jersey City
New Jersey USA

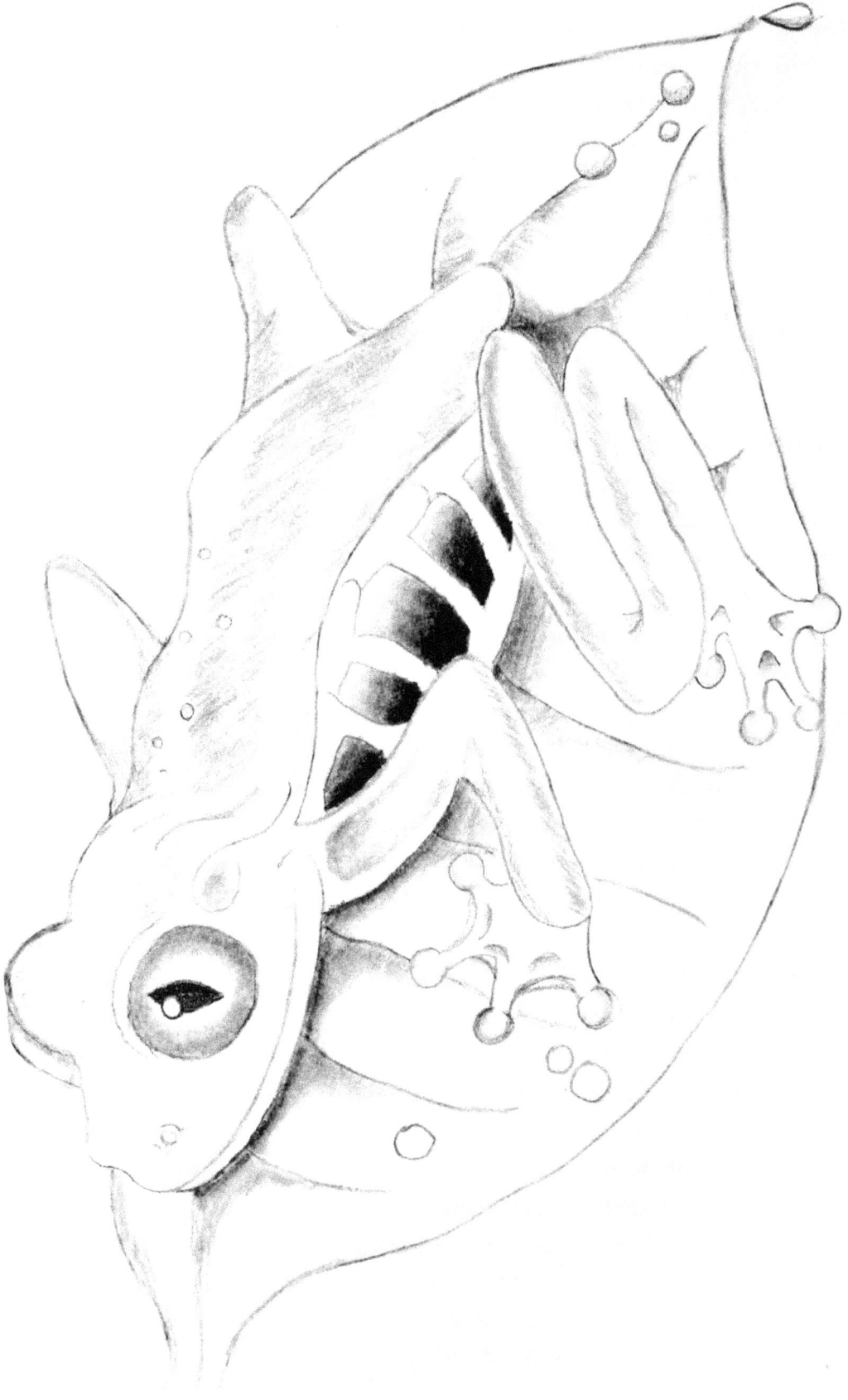

Esmeralda Garcia

Even though frogs do not have external ears they can hear both in the air and below water. Their eardrums are covered by circular areas of skin just behind their eyes.

Darius Lim Wei Chen

9 years old
Singapore

My Fat Fox

My Fat Fox is a small independent publisher of books and digital media. We are in love with our world and hope to encourage others to fall in love with it too.

More from My Fat Fox

Endangered Lizards Colouring Book
Endangered Frogs Colouring Book
Illustrated by Jay Manchand

Colour to Save the Ocean – Book One
Colour to Save the Ocean – Book Two
Illustrated by Kasia Niemczynska

Color and Save the Ocean – Book One
Wildlife Rescue Color and Learn - Costa Rica - For SIBU Wildlife Sanctuary
Party Animals Coloring Book – Moluccan Cockatoos - Mollywood
Illustrated by Karin Hoppe Holloway

Color Funny Doodles – Book One – Humorous
Color Funny Doodles – Book Two – Beautiful
Illustrated by Hartmut Jager

Where Do the Swallows Go?
Endangered Animals Colouring Book - UK Amphibians and Reptiles
Illustrated by Cassie Herschel-Shorland

Alan the Hedgehog (as Super Alan) in Colour Me Alan!
Illustrated by Jon Hitchman

Visit **www.myfatfox.co.uk** for competitions, news and information on our latest publications. All our Earth Art Colouring Books will soon also be available as Earth Art Apps.

www.ingramcontent.com/pod-product-compliance
Lightning Source LLC
Chambersburg PA
CBHW081723270326
41933CB00017B/3269